Bringing up Responsible Teenagers

A guide to managing conflict and getting on better with your teenager

JOHN SHARRY

VERITAS

Published 2001 by
Veritas Publications
7/8 Lower Abbey Street
Dublin 1

ISBN 1 85390 557 7

Acknowledgements
I would like to thank the hundreds of parents and teenagers that I have had the
privilege to work with over the years, who have taught me everything I know
about good parenting. This book reflects their struggles, their triumphs and
above all their wisdom – John Sharry

Design: Bill Bolger
Cartoons: John Byrne
Printed in the Republic of Ireland by Betaprint Ltd, Dublin

Veritas books are printed on paper made from the wood pulp of managed
forests. For every tree felled, at least one tree is planted, thereby renewing
natural resources.

Contents

A Stormy Time – Becoming a Parent of a Teenager

He just doesn't listen anymore and is so secretive and moody. He thinks that we [his parents] are for the birds and just wants to be with his friends all the time.

She's become so argumentative and abusive. Anytime we ask her to do anything she starts world war three in the house.

Becoming a parent of a teenager can be a troubled time. The young open child who chatted happily to you can suddenly become this argumentative and resentful teenager who challenges everything you say. Teenagers can become secretive and suspicious and you can feel redundant and locked out of their lives. In addition, you can be full of fears for your teenager. There are so many pressures on teenagers to be involved in drugs and alcohol or to become sexually active at too young an age. With their increasing independence, you can also fear for their safety, worrying that they might be attacked or placed in very unsafe situations. You struggle with setting boundaries and limits with a teenager who can resent your authority as a parent. Michael and Terri Quinn[1] describe how the crisis of children

1 Quinn & Quinn, 1988

becoming teenagers can hit parents at a difficult time. Parents are usually in their forties or fifties at the time and may be going through their own midlife crisis. At this stage of life parents are often wondering about the direction of their own lives and careers, sometimes feeling that life has passed them by. Having teenagers who seem to have endless opportunities and who appear ungrateful can stir up a lot of emotion in parents, even causing them to feel envious. Alternatively, parents may be looking forward to a quieter period in their life, only for this to be rudely disturbed by the arrival of a noisy and demanding teenager. In this context, it is understandable for parents to react negatively to this stormy period, to lose sight of the bigger picture and miss out on the enjoyable aspects of parenting a teenager.

IT'S DIFFICULT FOR TEENAGERS TOO

The transition from child to adult is difficult for teenagers also. So many changes occur in these short years that it is not surprising that they feel at times confused, frightened and lacking in confidence. Physically, their bodies grow and change in ways that might make them feel awkward and self-conscious. Emotionally, they can be subject to great mood swings as they discover the range of human emotions. From intense feelings of love and infatuation to anger and hatred, teenage emotional life can be like a roller-coaster. Physically, teenagers become fully developed and can experience intense sexual feelings that can be alarming to them, especially if they have no one to talk to about what is going on. Intellectually, teenagers also make great gains,

2

being able to analyse things and to develop their own opinions and views. They can begin to see the inadequacies in the parental world (and often are very eloquent in pointing this out!) and wonder about their role and meaning in life.

Teenagers are under pressures, some of which are greater than in previous years, and need the support of their parents more than ever.

NAVIGATING THE TEENAGE STORM

When facing the crisis of the teenage years, many parents react by trying to take control. They may become authoritarian and strict, battling with their teenagers to ensure they tow the line. Alternatively, other parents avoid their teenagers' problems and back down from every conflict, effectively giving up at trying to influence their teenagers or to be involved in their lives. Both these approaches are problematic: the young person with authoritarian parents may rebel even more strongly, escalating the conflict, or they may go 'underground' with their problems, hiding more things from their parents. The teenager with permissive parents may feel uncared for and neglected and, without parental supervision, get involved in out-of-control and unsafe behaviours. Both approaches rob teenagers of having involved parents who can support them through the difficulties they face.

3

This booklet aims to describe a 'middle way' approach to parenting that shows how you can stay supportively involved in your teenagers' lives while also being firm to ensure that they learn to take responsibility for their actions. The aim is to help teenagers grow into confident adults who are separate and independent but also appropriately connected to their family and able to form their own intimate relationships in the future.

Many writers describe family life and especially parenting a teenager as being like embarking on a plane journey together.[2] With a young child, the parent is in the pilot's seat, navigating the plane and in charge of the controls. As a child gets older, a good parent allows the child into the cockpit and begins to teach him how to operate the controls. As the child becomes a teenager, he begins to take the first steps of flying his own plane. The parent's role now becomes the important one of 'co-pilot', with the teenager slowly trying out his new skills. The 'co-pilot' is there for the teenager, offering encouragement and guidance, letting him learn from mistakes and achievements, teaching him slowly how to be a responsible pilot. Often this is difficult for families. Many parents fear that the child will not be able to fly safely and they battle with their child to take back the controls, insisting that he does not fly his own plane. Other parents do not give children any lessons at all, letting them learn the skills of flying from other people, such as their school friends or from the television. However, a good parent realises that the aim of the journey is to teach the teenager how to fly his own plane in the future and that it is far better that he learns this with his parents as supportive, involved co-pilots. A good co-pilot has faith in the trainee pilot's ability and is there actively to support him in the crucial job of flying the plane.

2 Covey, 1997; Nelson & Lott, 2000

SON –
THIS IS A
CHANCE FOR
YOU AND I
TO EXPERIENCE
SUBSTANTIAL
GROWTH
IN OUR
RELATIONSHIP...

GREAT – CAN WE
START WITH
MORE POCKET
MONEY ?

A Time of Opportunity

While acknowledging the strife and difficulties involved in bringing up a teenager, this book also suggests that parents seek out the positive and brighter side of parenting a teenager. Rather than seeing the teenage years as solely problem years, try to see them as full of opportunity. During these years parents have the opportunity to form a different relationship with their child, one that is more adult and equal. Teenage rebellion is not a personal attack on your authority but a necessary stage for teenagers to go through as they forge their separate identity. If you remain curious and interested in this process, you can help them think through their values and ideas. By staying involved in your teenagers' lives you can get to know them in a different light – as young adults rather than children. Many parents report how satisfying it can be to begin to have adult conversations with their teenagers. In addition, by staying involved you can share in their achievements and discoveries as they mature and grow up. You can appreciate and enjoy their excitement as they face a world full of opportunity and you can have the pleasure of being one of their closest supports as they take on the world. In the difficult times, try to remember that parenting is a long-term task. By staying involved and being firm when needed, you can chart a course through the difficult times so that you can be there as your teenagers grow into young adults of whom you can be proud.

NINE STEPS TO GETTING ALONG WITH TEENAGERS

In the following pages we look at nine principles which, if applied over time, can make a real difference in helping you get along with your teenager and in managing conflict in your family relationships. The principles are derived from a parenting course (the Parents Plus Families and Adolescents Programme), which is offered in many clinics throughout Ireland. The principles can be viewed as nine steps that you can follow one by one over the next few weeks. Most of the ideas will be familiar to you and be recognised as good, positive habits of parenting to which we all aspire. While the ideas are well researched as useful to most families, none apply in every situation and in every context. Each family is different, and it is parents who know their children and their families best. I encourage you in the booklet to reflect on what works for you as a parent and to adapt the ideas and suggestions to your own unique family situation. While I encourage you to try new things out, trust your own gut instinct to lead you to what's best for you and your family.

Step One – Pressing the Pause Button

It's the last straw for Pete when his fourteen-year-old son arrives home hours late after specifically promising to be in on time. Pete confronts him angrily, asking 'Where the hell have you been?' The son in return becomes defensive and angry and tells his father to mind his own business. The confrontation escalates and the son storms off to his room. Pete is left wondering what has happened between them.

Teenagers are at a time of life when they are separating from their parents. They are becoming their own people, with different ideas and values. Though this is healthy, it can bring them into conflict with their parents and lead to a stormy time for all. As we discussed in the last section, this period can be difficult for parents. Teenagers can become challenging and demanding. At times they can become disrespectful and even abusive to their parents. It is not surprising that parents, hurt and bewildered by these exchanges, can react negatively by criticising, lecturing, rowing and even lashing out at their teenagers. This can lead to unpleasant scenes, like that described above, leaving both teenager and parent upset and hurt.

PRESSING THE PAUSE BUTTON

So how can a parent handle this conflict? How can you stop things from escalating to a full-blown row? The first thing you can do is press the pause button. Rather than reacting to a situation or 'flying off the handle', pause and ask yourself the following questions:

● What is the best way to manage this situation?
● What way do I want to respond?
● What result do I want?

In conflictual situations, pressing the pause button may mean taking a deep breath and calming down when you feel yourself getting angry or about to react to a situation. It can be best not to continue the argument, which may lead to hurtful things being said, and to set a time later to talk things through when everyone is calmer. Consider now how Pete in the example above might have pressed the pause button.

> *When his son came in late, Pete found himself getting very angry, but he quickly noticed this. He took a deep breath and said, 'Look son, I'm just too upset and angry to talk now. Go to your room and we will talk tomorrow.' The son went off in a huff, but a serious row was averted. Pete sat down and collected himself, thinking what was the best way to approach his son about his being late. He decided on a way and then sat down with him at a later time when both were calm.*

WHEN TEENAGERS ARE DISRESPECTFUL

Pressing the pause button can also be helpful when teenagers become abusive and disrespectful to parents. Rather than tolerating the teenager's abuse or responding with a few choice words of your own, you can 'pause the row' by refusing to participate anymore and waiting for a better time to resolve the conflict. Consider the example below:

> *When Alice asked her daughter to stay in one evening, she exploded abusively, telling her mother to 'back off' and 'stop messing up my life'. Though Alice was hurt and tempted to respond angrily, she pressed the pause button. She calmly said 'Look, I'm not happy with you speaking to me in this way. When you can talk civilly, then I'll listen.' The daughter continued to protest and Alice repeated what she had just said and walked away. Away from the situation Alice thought about what to do and the daughter calmed down. An hour later her daughter approached her and the two of them sat down and talked. Alice calmly explained how hurt she was and the daughter apologised. Together they negotiated a compromise about going out.*

By pressing the pause button, Alice 'nipped the argument in the bud' and avoided the row escalating to a point where hurtful and damaging things were said. By not returning her daughter's abuse, Alice not only made it more likely that a more constructive conversation could take place later, but she also taught her daughter an important lesson about how to remain respectful and calm even in a difficult situation.

DON'T WAIT FOR A ROW – PRESS THE PAUSE BUTTON IN ADVANCE!

You don't have to wait until you are in the middle of a row to press the pause button and think through how you want to manage a conflict or how you want to be as a parent. In fact, the more often you sit down (either by yourself or with your partner or a trusted friend) to reflect on your parenting and to plan how you are going to handle situations, the better things are likely to be for yourself and your family. Good planning and communication can avoid many problems. For example, by taking time to plan with your teenagers the family holiday, a choice can be made that meets the preferences of everyone, and this can avoid resentment or a disastrous trip full of rows and conflict.

However, many parents caught up in busy schedules forget to give themselves 'thinking time' or forget to plan things in their families. The purpose of this book is to 'press the pause button' in your busy parenting schedule and to give you 'thinking time'. Most of the exercises and suggestions in the book are about 'pausing' by yourself or with your children to think and talk about what way you want to be as a family. Some things to remember in reflecting how you might approach problems with your teenagers are:

1. Focus on your goal and what you want to happen (what way do you want to be as a parent, couple, family?).
2. Focus on what you can do (rather than waiting for your teenager to change, what can you do to help her change or to make the situation better?).
3. Remember what has worked with your teenager in the past (for example, you may remember that chatting after dinner is more effective) and try to do this again.
4. If something isn't working, try something different.

PRESSING THE PAUSE BUTTON IN ADVANCE – EXAMPLES
- Rather than being authoritarian when her son refused to do something, Jean decided to take some time to listen to his point of view and then try to reach a compromise.
- Arthur realised that it was a 'bad time' to harangue his daughter with questions about how school went the minute she came in from school and was tired, and remembered that a better time was later, after dinner, when everyone was relaxed.
- Instead of jumping in to referee when his two sons got into a squabble, Roy decided to back off, saying to them, 'Listen, the two of you are old enough to sort your disagreements out.'
- Julie used to constantly nag her daughter to clean her room, to no avail. She decided to pay no attention to it anymore, but told her daughter that she would only get her full pocket money if she cleaned her room.

TIPS FOR GOING FORWARD
1. Press the pause button when faced with rows and arguments. Step back and think how you want to respond.
2. Think of a particular problem that occurs in your family and plan what you might do differently to make a difference.
3. Sit down and make a list of your goals. What way do you want to be as a parent, as a couple, as a family? What is important? Maybe start a discussion with others in the family.

Step Two – Connecting with your Teenager

When my children got older, I felt redundant. They had their own friends and lives. It became harder to understand them.

PARENTS MATTER

Often parents have the sense of being out of touch with their teenager. Teenagers get caught up with their own friends and interests, and it is easy to feel distant from them and that you don't matter to them anymore. Yet teenagers still really need their parents. Though they are growing up and separating from the family, they still need support, guidance and encouragement. They need parents who remain involved and interested in their lives. Young people need adults who can be there to coach them and act as their 'co-pilot' as they negotiate the problems they face in their lives. If you are unsure about the importance of your role in your teenager's life, you only have to consider the extensive research showing that teenagers whose parents stay connected and supportively involved in their lives are much more likely to grow into healthy, successful adults with fewer problems.[3] Researchers have also found that children whose parents discuss issues such as drugs with them are 36 per cent less likely to experiment with drugs than children whose parents do not have these discussions.

GUESS WHAT? I KNOW YOUR FAVOURITE DINNER!

BIG DEAL! WHEN YOU KNOW BRAD PITT'S FAVOURITE DINNER, I'LL BE IMPRESSED!

3 Covey, 1997

Staying involved in your teenagers' lives or having a connection with them does not mean knowing everything about them or learning things so you can control them. Teenagers need their privacy and distance and it would be inappropriate for them to reveal all their innermost secrets to their parents. Rather, having a connection with teenagers is about knowing the ordinary details in their lives that are important to them, such as the names of their friends, their routine at school, the position of their team in the league, what their favourite dinner is, etc. When you know these mundane and ordinary details about your teenagers' lives, not only does it mean that you are sharing in their lives, but it gives you an opportunity to influence them positively about other important matters such as drug-taking and safety.

BUILDING A CONNECTION WITH YOUR TEENAGER

So how do you get through to teenagers? How do you reach out to them when they appear withdrawn and moody? This is often not easy, as there can be a great gap between parents and teenagers in terms of interests and concerns. Building a connection and a good relationship with your teenager takes effort and it is not something that can be done overnight, but rather is the result of careful emotional investment of time and energy. There are a number of ideas that can help.

SET TIME ASIDE TO BE WITH YOUR TEENAGER

Building a connection with a child or teenager is not something that can be rushed or fitted into a busy schedule. The most important decision you can make is to set time aside when you can talk and be with your teenager in a relaxed way. This does not have to be a special activity or trip (though these can help, as we shall see in Step Three). Mundane ordinary activities such as watching TV together, driving to school, mealtimes, washing up together, all can become activities where parent and child are happily chatting to one another.

> *Rob found the drive to work in the morning when he dropped his son to school a real stress. They would always be late and tempers could be frayed in the traffic. As a result, he changed his schedule so as to have more time in the morning. This made the journey more relaxing, giving them time to spend together either chatting or listening to the radio. It became a time they both looked forward to.*

Some parents find routine events of the day particularly helpful times to talk and listen to their children, such as when they come in from school, at mealtimes, or late at night just before they go to bed. Many families agree to make some of these times special, such as Sunday dinner, when everyone makes an effort to be there.

GET TO KNOW SPECIFIC DETAILS ABOUT YOUR TEENAGER'S WORLD

Parents who are involved in their children's lives know countless ordinary details about their lives and what is important to them. They take an interest in their hobbies and make a point of remembering their friends' names. They are curious about what their children think and feel about things, especially things that are important to them. Gaining this knowledge of your child's life takes time but it really shows in the quality of interaction between parent and child. Consider the example below:

Joan would make a special effort to be available to her children when they came in from school. She would stop any work she was doing and sit down with her children over a cup of tea. She made sure there would be time and space for everyone to say how their day went. Joan made a point to ask specifically what went on for them during the day and she always remembered to ask about important things such as football matches or trips. This special time after school became a really important family ritual that Joan and the children looked forward to.

BE ENCOURAGING

Teenagers are often insecure and struggling with many pressures at school and from friends. The argumentative or sulky moods are only a front and they need more than ever the support and encouragement of their parents. It is important that this encouragement be given in a genuine way, as teenagers will be the first to shrug off any attention they consider to be 'phoney' or manipulative. Generally, encouragement works best with teenagers if it is matter of fact rather than 'over the top', and if it is specific and clear (whereby you clearly name what you are pleased about and how you feel about it). Remember, each teenager is different; what gets through with one teenager will not work for another. What is important is that you find a way of providing encouragement to your teenager about routine, everyday activities. Giving compliments to teenagers in a genuine way that gets through to them can make a difference.

- Noticing if your teenager tries harder at school work.
- Casually thanking your teenager when he does a chore rather than taking it for granted.
- Complimenting teenagers on their appearance or what they're wearing.

Going out of your way to look for positive things does not come easily to most of us. We are not used to it, and praise can be hard to give, particularly when there has been conflict or things have not been going well with a child for some time. But that is probably the most important time to be positive and to notice even small signs of improvement. For example, if your teenager is normally grumpy with visitors, but on one occasion, behaves more positively, you could say, 'I appreciate it when you talk with my friends, it means a lot to me when you take an interest.' Or if a teenager normally gets into a row with his sister, but on one occasion walks away, you could say, 'I was impressed with how you handled things with your sister earlier. You didn't get wound up and avoided a row.'

RESPONDING TO YOUR TEENAGER'S INITIATIVE

One of the greatest opportunities to connect with teenagers is to respond to any initiatives they make to talk with or connect with you. Often they choose inopportune times, when you're busy or when you're tired or just about to go out and do something yourself. However, it's worth weighing up in these situations what is really important – the tasks you're busy with or your relationship with your teenager. While you can sometimes postpone responding to your teenager, it can be really helpful to respond there and then, especially if your teenager does not usually open up or try to make a connection with you. It can be a case of making sure to 'seize the opportunity'. Consider the following examples:

- If your son asks for help with homework and you're busy, try to give a little bit of time and then set aside another time to help.
- If your daughter suddenly opens up one night because her boyfriend split up with her, this might be a time to postpone going to bed and to stay up and listen.
- If your son wants to watch a favourite TV programme and you're reading, it might be a good idea to postpone your reading and to watch the programme with him.
- If your daughter asks you a personal question when you're reading the newspaper, you can put down the newspaper for a few minutes and try to listen and answer the question.
- If your son asks you for a lift, rather than lecturing him about 'not being his chauffeur', use the journey as an opportunity to listen and talk to him.

TIPS FOR GOING FORWARD

1. Set aside a relaxed time to talk with your teenager, when the two of you can sit and chat.
2. Make a list of all the specific, mundane details you know about your teenager (friends, interests, school, likes/dislikes, etc.). Make an effort to fill any gaps you notice, by taking a real interest in your teenager's life next week (Remember to 'go slow', as your teenager may only open up slowly).
3. Be really encouraging of your teenager. Go out of your way to notice any things he does that you like or you're proud of and make sure to tell him this.
4. Be sure to respond to any attempts your teenager makes to connect or talk to you.

Step Three – Getting to Know Your Teenager

BEING A TEENAGER

As a parent, it's easy to forget what it is like to be a teenager. You can find yourself being critical of the younger generation, complaining about their laziness or lack of respect for older people. You can just see their moodiness as a burden and something you can't understand. However, what young people really need is their parents' understanding. They are often very critical of themselves, feeling awkward and having low self-esteem. They need to know that you are on their side. To appreciate what it is like in your teenager's shoes, it can help to remember what it was like for you as a teenager when you were growing up. To do this, I suggest you take a few minutes with the following exercise.

REMEMBERING BEING A TEENAGER

1. Take a few moments out from your routine so that you can be alone, with time to think and reflect.
2. Close your eyes and take a few deep breaths to relax.
3. Begin to recall what it was like when you were ten or eleven years old. Pick out specific events or people that signify this time for you. Focus on recalling specific details (how you were feeling, what people were saying, what things looked like then, etc.).
4. When you're ready, begin to move forward in time to when you were fifteen or sixteen (in the middle of your teen years) and begin to recall what things were like for you then. Once again, recall specific events and people in as much detail as possible.
5. When you are ready, move forward again to the present day and back to the room you're in.
6. Think about what you noticed about your 'journey' through time. It can help to write things down in a journal or to talk to someone about what you have noticed or remembered, such as your partner. This can be a good exercise to do as a couple.

The above exercise can be very powerful in getting you in touch with your own teenage years. It can be a difficult exercise as you can recall sad memories, or it can be mixed as you recall good and bad memories. As a parent doing the exercise, it can make you realise some of the issues that your own teenager is going through. Though there are many differences between being a teenager nowadays and a generation ago (for example, it is true to say that teenagers have more freedom now and there is wider availability of drugs), many of the issues are the same. By remembering these common issues and concerns, you have made another step in understanding and connecting with your teenager.

WHAT TEENAGERS THINK ABOUT

So what do teenagers think about? What issues are important to them and what concerns press upon their minds? Below are the sorts of worries that teenagers have reported as most concerning them:

1. Will I make friends or will anyone like me?
2. Will anyone fancy me or ask me out?
3. How come I don't fit in with others?
4. What should I do about drugs and alcohol?
5. Will I do okay in the class exams?
6. Will I ever get a decent job?
7. What should I do with my life?
8. How can I please my parents/get them off my back?

Teenagers also tend to have strong views about how they should be parented and about what they want from their parents:

1. They want their parents to trust them and have faith in them.
2. They want privacy. They want to talk to their parents about some things but they don't want to tell them everything.

3. They want to be treated fairly. Justice and fair play are really important to them.

GETTING TO KNOW YOUR TEENAGER

As a parent, the best thing you can do to get alongside your teenager, so that you can be a positive influence in their life, is to go out of your way to understand them and to know their world. Rules and discipline require teenagers to co-operate voluntarily and thus are only possible when you have established a good relationship. Below are a number of things you can do to make a difference to your relationship with your teenager:

BE INTERESTED

Be genuinely interested in your teenagers and all they do. You want to know them, not because you want to control them, but because you genuinely want to get to know their world. You want to know their opinions, views and feelings. You want to understand why they love computer games so much, or what they see in football, so that you can share in this with them. This often requires suspending your critical judgements of their interests and hobbies and reaching out to understand them. For example, rather than always criticising a TV programme your daughter watches, make an effort to suspend judgement, watch it with her, and then debate the issues with her, listening to her point of view first. Let your teenager teach you about her interests and what it is like to be living in the teenage world. See yourself as a curious, respectful traveller in a foreign land (of adolescence!) rather than being a critical tourist! Rather than simply restricting your son's use of the Internet, let him teach you how to use it and show you the benefits and opportunities it provides. By learning about it yourself, you are in a better position to open a debate about the problems of safety or excessive use. You may be surprised to find that your teenager has already thought about many of the issues involved. Your job then becomes one of a supportive coach, helping him think things through further and make decisions.

SPEND ONE-TO-ONE TIME WITH YOUR TEENAGER

The best way to build a trusting close relationship with your teenager is to ensure that you have one-to-one quality time together, with no interruptions. While this can be difficult with teenagers who appear little interested in spending time with their parents, and when parents are busy with their own lives, time alone with your teenagers is still the best way to get to know them and stay involved with their lives. There are many things you can do to achieve this and often it is best to plan in advance to find activities that you enjoy doing together.

- Watching a favourite TV programme
- Doing homework
- Shopping together
- Playing cards
- Playing sport
- Baking/cooking
- Walking the dog
- Following a football team
- Making something (e.g. a craft)
- Walking, cycling
- Camping
- Doing a course together
- Fishing
- Working on the computer

MAKE A DECISION TO GET TO KNOW YOUR TEENAGER

Often getting to know your teenager isn't something that just happens. The generation gap can be quite large and requires an effort on the part of the parent to bridge it. This is especially the case when parents feel out of touch with their teenagers or if there has been a lot of conflict. Consider the two examples of parents below:

Richard found his fourteen-year-old son particularly grumpy and moody and he felt out of touch with him. So he looked to find an activity they could do together. The son was really interested in football, though Rob thought it was a waste of time. But he decided to take an interest in football and began to attend matches with his son. Slowly he discovered and began to share his son's love for the sport. The weekly football trip soon became their regular weekend outing and a real bond developed between them.

Sue found herself in constant battles with her daughter over school work. She was worried that they had nothing in common. However, when she thought about it she remembered that they both shared an interest in films. So as a treat she planned a special movie night, when the two of them would select a movie and go together, and round off the evening in a coffee shop. This worked well, as they always had a great chat about the movie and other things over coffee.

BE PREPARED TO SHARE YOUR OWN EXPERIENCES

Generally, teenagers love when parents are prepared to share their own honest feelings and experiences rather than just give lectures and advice. For example, rather than preaching to your son about the virtues of hard work in school or lecturing to him about the dangers of teenage sex, maybe share with him your own personal struggles in school or your own teenage worries about relationships and meeting the opposite sex. It can be helpful to share with your teenager the results of the remembering exercise at the beginning of this section. Sharing your own honest feelings and experiences can be really helpful in improving your relationship with your teenager. Consider the example from a mother below:

I was always concerned about my daughter not studying and going out all the time and this would lead to a lot of conflict. Things changed when we were away together one weekend and I told her honestly about my own school experience. I had been taken out of school early by my parents to work and always resented not having an opportunity to go to college. Talking to her made me realise how part of my pressure on my daughter was to do with my own lack of fulfilment. My daughter was very understanding when I told her this and she opened up about the pressures she had in school, which were different to mine. We began to understand one another and have been much closer as a result.

SPEND FAMILY TIME TOGETHER

Another way to get to know your teenager and to improve family life in general is to ensure that there are regular times when the whole family spends quality time together. This can include special activities such as a day-trip together, going on a picnic, or staying in for a special movie night. Many families organise a special family night (usually following a family meeting, see Step Eight) when everyone stays in, perhaps to share a meal together or a special family activity such as a game, telling stories, playing music, or simply spending time with one another.

TIPS FOR GOING FORWARD

1. Plan to do an activity or take up a hobby that you can share with your teenager.
2. Plan an enjoyable family event or set aside family time, which everyone, including your teenagers, can enjoy and take part in.

Step Four – Communicating Effectively – Listening and Speaking Up

ACTIVE LISTENING

Most parents agree that listening to children is really important. Some writers in the field actually rate listening as the most important parenting skill of all. This is because it helps parents to both understand and get alongside their teenagers and it also helps resolve conflict and carry out discipline firmly. Yet despite this, very few of us get any training in how to listen. It is something we just pick up as we go along and sometimes we can find it very difficult, especially when we have strong views about what we want to happen for our teenagers.

Active listening involves great effort. It involves stepping out of your own shoes into those of another person. It involves moving to see the world as they see it and to appreciate the feelings they have towards it. It is about going that extra distance to understand their point of view. When faced by your child doing something you strongly disagree with, a good indicator that you have understood empathetically is when you appreciate that you might have committed the same error if you had been in their shoes or faced their set of circumstances.

SO HOW DO YOU ACTIVELY LISTEN?

Active listening is very different than the many other ways we might communicate with teenagers, such as giving advice, criticising, or coaching (all useful skills at times but not when we are actively listening to understand a child's feelings). Consider the following responses to a teenager:

Paul *(Upset)*: James just turned the TV over to his channel.
Parent: Well, I'm sure it was his turn. *(Arguing)*
            You shouldn't be watching so much TV. *(Criticism)*
            Why don't you just do something else? *(Advice)*
            Oh, don't worry, it's not so bad. *(Coaching)*
            Let me go and talk to James. *(Rescuing)*

Instead, active listening is something quite different. It involves skills such as the following:
● Genuinely trying to understand.
● Acknowledging what the other person is feeling.
● Repeating what the other person has said, to check you have understood.
● Giving full attention via your body language and eye contact.
● Encouraging the other person to continue by nodding, being silent, repeating the last word they have said, asking gentle questions, etc.

Consider now some alternative listening responses:

Paul *(Upset)*: James just turned the TV over to his channel.
Parent: Sounds like you are upset. Sit down and tell me what happened. *(Picking up on feelings and encouraging child to say more)*
            I'm sorry, I know how much you like watching that programme. *(Acknowledging feelings)*

In the above examples the parent is validating the child's feelings and attempting to see the problem from his point of view. Sometimes, simply repeating what the child has said, or nodding encouragingly, can be sufficient to help the child feel listened to and to encourage him to express more.

It is important to remember that good listening can't be reduced to a set of techniques (If you do find yourself 'parroting' techniques, your teenager will soon point this out to you). What counts is your genuine attempt to understand and appreciate the other's point of view. You have listened effectively when the other person feels understood, that you don't judge them, and that you are on their side.

LISTENING CHANGES YOU

When we empathetically listen to another person we open ourselves to be influenced by them. We allow ourselves to be changed and transform the nature of our relationship with the other person. Consider the following example from a father:

I always considered myself to have a good relationship with my two teenage sons. I thought everyone enjoyed the joking and good-natured banter that would go on between us. That was until the youngest of the two exploded one day over very little. I gave him what for, but I could see something was really bugging him so I went back to him and listened. He told me how he had always felt embarrassed and humiliated by the banter and the teasing. I began to hear how this had really damaged him. I can't tell you how painful this was to hear. But it marked a pivotal point in our relationship. One year on we now have a much closer and adult relationship. I am really glad now that I decided to listen that day.

26

SPEAKING UP

We've talked about the importance of actively listening to teenagers when they feel strongly about something. It is equally important that parents communicate their own feelings when they feel strongly about something. Teenagers need parents who don't go along with everything they say or who always agree with them. They need parents who are prepared to state their own views and to communicate their values and opinions. How this is done makes a big difference. Skilled communicators always listen first before speaking up with their own point of view. Often people get the order of this the wrong way round: they attempt to get their point of view across before listening to the other person. This can lead to a lot of conflict. When we understand another person's point of view and have acknowledged their feelings, they are far more likely to be open to listen to us. Expressing your views and concerns also requires skill and tact. Often parents fall into the traps of blaming, criticising or not acknowledging their own feelings. Speaking up respectfully involves:

1. Remaining calm and positive.
2. Taking responsibility for your feelings by using an 'I' message, for example, 'I feel upset' rather than 'you made me upset'.
3. Expressing your positive intentions and concerns such as 'I want you to be safe'.
4. Focusing on what you want to happen, for example, saying 'I want you to tell me when you're late'.

EXAMPLES OF INEFFECTIVE AND EFFECTIVE SPEAKING UP

Ineffective: What the hell do you think you are playing at staying out so late? You've really upset me.
(Attacking and blaming 'you' message)

Effective: I worry about you going out late at night, especially when it is dark. You see, I want you to be safe.
(Expresses feelings as a positive concern using an 'I' message)

Ineffective: Is there something wrong with you that you don't see this mess? You and your friends are so inconsiderate.
(Sarcastic, blaming)

Effective: Listen, I like it when your friends come round, but I get frustrated if they leave the place in a mess. I'd really like it if they tidied up after themselves.
(States positive first, acknowledges own feelings of frustration and then makes a clear reasonable request)

Ineffective: You're talking rubbish now. Of course it's always wrong for teenagers at school to get involved in a sexual relationship.
(Argumentative, attacking)

Effective: My own view is that teenagers at school are far too young to get involved in a sexual relationship.
(Respectful offering of parents view/value)

TIPS FOR GOING FORWARD

1. Practise communicating well with your teenagers and other family members. When they feel strongly about something, make a real attempt to actively listen and to understand their point of view.

2. Practise speaking up respectfully to your teenagers, offering your view in a calm, assertive way.

Step Five – Managing Conflict

Fifteen-year-old Lisa arrives home from school one day to drop the bombshell to her father, Bill, that she's had enough and that she has decided to leave school. Bill, who is just home after a stressful day at work, flies off the handle saying she's talking nonsense, that she is far too young even to consider leaving school. Lisa storms off, slamming a door, saying she's going to leave anyway.

Conflicts such as the one described above are common in families with teenagers or older children. Teenagers are on the road to becoming independent from their parents and this can be a long process, with each 'step of independence' being hard-won as parent and child clash over rules. Adolescence is the time of life when young people need to separate and be different from their parents – they will often have different views on clothes, time-keeping, friends, money, the importance of school work. Though it can lead to conflict, the expression of these different views is healthy and helps young people grow up into confident adults.

DOES BEING A PARENT INEVITABLY INVOLVE CONFLICT WITH YOUR TEENAGERS?

YES – SO WHY FIGHT IT?

What is important is how conflict is managed in families. You want to have a family in which there is a healthy and respectful expression of differences, but you do not want excessive conflict, leading to constant rows, as this can make things worse and damage relationships.

In this section we look at how, as a parent, you can manage conflict between yourself and your teenager in a way that is respectful and positive and that offers the possibility of resolving the disagreements that caused the problems in the first place. We review ideas already covered in the book, especially in the last section, and consider how these can be applied specifically to resolving conflict.

1. Pressing the pause button.
2. Active listening.
3. Speaking up assertively

PRESSING THE PAUSE BUTTON

The behaviour of teenagers can be very provocative and challenging at times. In working out their own views, teenagers may reject values or ideas that are very important to their parents. For example, if you are a religious person, your teenager may refuse to go to church, or if cooking is important to you, your teenager might reject your food and choose an 'alternative diet', or if education is important to you, your teenager may threaten to drop out of school. Teenagers can know what buttons to push to get you going and this can cause great conflict. However, the first step to combat this is to press your own pause button. Rather than reacting angrily, take some time out to understand what is going on. Instead of taking your teenagers' behaviour personally, understand it as part of their growing up into being adults. Remember, if you do resort to lecturing or angry exchanges, you may inadvertently fan the flames of the rebellion.

Pressing the pause button gives you time to think through the best way to respond. Even if there has been a row or if you have over-reacted, pressing the pause button gives you an opportunity to apologise and start again. In the example at the beginning of this section, Lisa's father Bill could recover after the row, by taking some time for himself to reflect about what was going on, then to approach Lisa later at a good time, apologising for 'flying off the handle', and finally to ask her to start again and tell him what happened.

ACTIVE LISTENING

In conflict situations between parent and teenager, emotions are likely to be running high. Conflicts are at their strongest when both parent and teenager feel really strongly, but differently, about something. In the above example, Lisa may be feeling really hopeless about her school, thinking it has no benefit to her. Her father on the other hand may believe strongly that teenagers should finish school and may feel scared at the prospect of her leaving early. In the context of their strong but different feelings, it is understandable that Bill may get angry and Lisa may storm off. However, until they find a way of listening to one another they are unlikely to resolve the disagreement.

Active listening isn't easy. It is especially hard when there is serious conflict such as that between Bill and Lisa. However, these are the times when active listening is especially useful. If you don't listen, the conflict doesn't disappear, in fact it may worsen, as your teenager is likely to feel hurt and close up and not tell you what is really going on with her. Consider the above example now continued below, where Bill goes out of his way to listen to Lisa's feelings and to understand her point of view:

Bill:	*(Pauses and takes a deep breath)* Look, I'm sorry, let me try to understand.
Lisa:	School is wrecking my head. I'm always in trouble. Even when I try, the teachers don't notice.
Bill:	I see.
Lisa:	Yeah, each day I go in I feel they're picking on me. I'd be better off leaving and getting work.
Bill:	You've been having a real hard time at school recently.

Lisa: Yeah I have.

                (Father silently nods and puts arm around daughter's shoulder, who shows a small response, suggesting she is beginning to feel understood)

Lisa: That's why I want to leave. I'd be much better leaving and getting a job somewhere. *(Pause)*

Bill: Mmmh, I don't think I've appreciated how much of a struggle school has been for you, I guess, because I've always wanted it to go well for you. I need to think about what you are saying. Can we talk later, because it is a very important issue?

Lisa: Yeah.

In the above conversation, Bill is making a real attempt to listen to his daughter, but it is hard for him. It is hard for him to take on board his daughter's struggles in school and thus her wish to leave, probably because these views run counter to his strongly held opinion about the importance of completing education. However, if he truly wants to support his daughter's education, he first has to become her ally. He first has to hear about his daughter's difficulties in school before he can go on to help her solve the problem (In Step Eight we will look at possible ways of developing solutions).

When your teenager feels strongly about something, these are really opportunities in disguise. By really listening at these times, you have the opportunity to deeply connect with your teenager and to transform your relationship with her.

SPEAKING UP ASSERTIVELY

While listening is usually the best way to start during a conflict, it is also important for parents to speak up and communicate their own point of view. However, the way this is done makes a real difference. It is important not to come across as aggressive, where you intimidate or inadvertently attack your teenager.

. Equally, it is important not to be passive, where you don't get your view across for fear of upsetting your teenager, or you back down too easily and let your teenager walk all over you. Rather, the aim is to speak up assertively, whereby you communicate respectfully and calmly what you feel and think, making sure to express your positive intentions and feelings.

Even during serious conflicts and problems between parent and child, active listening and speaking up assertively are the best ways to begin to resolve them. Consider the next example, where a mother tackles her son over the drugs she has found in his room. She has taken time to think about what she is going to say and has picked a good time to approach her son to discuss what she has found.

Mother:	Look, I've something very important to talk to you about.
Son:	What?
Mother:	I found this in your room *(Puts what looks like cannabis on the table. Son looks shocked)*
Mother:	I know it is cannabis.
Son: *(Outraged)*	What the hell were you doing in my room?
Mother: *(Calm)*	I was worried because of what the teacher said about you using drugs, so I decided to check.
Son:	You had no right to go into my room.
Mother: *(Respectfully)*	I'm sorry I had to, but I needed to check what the teacher said.
Son: *(Slumps in chair)*	Well, it's none of your business.
Mother:	It's because I'm very worried for you. I don't want you to use drugs.
Son:	It's only hash. It's no big deal.
Mother:	It is a big deal to me. I want you to be safe and well. *(Teen folds arms)*

Mother:	Listen to me. *(Teen turns)* We are going to have to talk about this and sort it out. *(The son sighs and sort of gives in, as if he's beginning to sense his mother's persistent concern for him.)*

In the last example the mother spoke up firmly and well. She had clearly thought through what she was going to say. Though it was a serious and worrying issue, she remained calm. She expressed her feelings clearly and positively, stating her concern for her son. Finally, she did not take the bait in rising to her son's anger and was persistent in getting her positive message through.

IN SUMMARY

Managing conflict is essentially about good, respectful communication. It is about making sure you are talking and discussing things openly, rather than simply fighting and arguing. It is about staying involved and appreciating differences and not withdrawing or avoiding conflict. The two most important communication skills are listening empathetically and speaking up respectfully. You want to understand the other person's point of view and help them understand you as well. Remember these two skills form the building blocks of resolving disagreements and when applied over time can resolve even the most serious conflict.

TIPS FOR GOING FORWARD

When you find yourself in a dispute next week, practise 1) pausing rather than reacting, 2) active listening before you respond, 3) respectfully speaking up and giving your point of view.

Step Six – Empowering Teenagers

As said before, parenting teenagers is a bit like teaching them to fly their own plane. During these years, the parent acts like a supportive co-pilot, ready to teach and support the 'trainee' pilot. Though it can be hard, you have to learn to relinquish the controls one by one and support your teenager as she learns to take responsibility. In addition, you have to remain sufficiently involved in your teenager's life so that she seeks out your support and accepts your influence. In other words, you may have to work very hard at staying connected with your teenager so that she allows you into the co-pilot's seat in the first place! (and so that she doesn't later push the 'ejector button' and sack you from the role before the job is complete!)

WHEN IS BEING THE PARENT OF A TEENAGER LIKE TRAINING A PILOT?

WHEN SIX OF HIS FRIENDS CRASH AT YOUR HOUSE FOR THE NIGHT!

Just as the long-term aim of the co-pilot is to empower their trainees to become fully qualified pilots, so the long-term aim of the parent is to empower their teenagers to be confident, capable adults who are responsible for their own lives. However, this is more difficult than it seems, and many parents fall into the trap of being 'disempowering' rather than 'empowering' parents.

DISEMPOWERING PARENTING

Below are three styles of disempowering parenting that you can easily fall into, despite the best of intentions. Each of these styles cultivates irresponsibility in teenagers and does not prepare them for the task of being an adult:

● *Over-protective Parent*
Doing everything for your teenagers, for example, waking them in the morning, making their breakfast and lunch, tidying up for them, washing their clothes, covering for them when they miss homework, etc.

● *Critical Parent*
Nagging, correcting, instructing teenagers over every task without giving them space and responsibility. For example, nagging them to do the lawn and then standing over them while they do it, even criticising their attempts.

● *Permissive Parent*
Giving your teenagers excessive 'space' so that you are uninvolved and have little influence in their lives (meaning they learn little from you).

EMPOWERING PARENTING

BE ENCOURAGING
Perhaps the most empowering thing you can do as a parent is to be supportive and encouraging. Begin to trust your teenagers and express your belief in their ability to succeed. Highlight and identify what they do right and the good qualities that they have. See yourself as a good coach in their lives. You cheerlead when they are successful, are a shoulder to cry on when they hit hard disappointments, and are there to chat to in the ordinary times. But you are always positively on their side. Even when they do wrong, you help them take responsibility, and you help

them learn, but you continue to support and encourage them. Perhaps the greatest gift we can give our children is to maintain an unwavering belief in them during the bad times or periods of discouragement.

LET TEENAGERS TAKE RESPONSIBILITY FOR HOUSEHOLD AND FAMILY TASKS

This suggestion should be welcome relief to overburdened parents who do everything for their teenagers – you do them no service by taking charge of their lives in this way. It robs them of a chance to learn important life skills and to develop a sense of pride in carrying out the jobs well. Doing everything for teenagers also disempowers them, because it inadvertently communicates to them that they are not capable of carrying out the tasks in the first place. During the teenage years you should hand over household and family tasks to them one by one so that they eventually take a fair adult responsibility in the running of a home. Michael and Terri Quinn have compiled a list of all the tasks that parents could hand over to teenagers. They recommend using it as a checklist that you can review periodically to see what else you can hand over and teach your teenager!

TASKS TO TEACH YOUR TEENAGER
- Weekly household shopping
- Choosing their own clothes
- Getting up in the morning
- Washing-up
- Mowing the grass
- Painting a room
- Paying bills
- Locking doors at night
- Cooking meals
- Cleaning the house
- Washing clothes
- Doing basic repairs

- Ironing
- Changing the oil in the car
- Mending an electric fuse
- Wiring an electric plug
- Caring for a younger child
- Cleaning the windows
- Planting flowers and vegetables
- Leading prayers
- Chopping firewood
- Settling their own squabbles

TEACH TEENAGERS TO MAKE DECISIONS IN THEIR OWN LIVES

Teaching teenagers to make decisions about their own lives is the most important task that parents can hand over. Parents should empower teenagers to begin to make decisions, such as how to manage their routine, what friends to have, what lifestyle to have, and what to do in the future. Rather than giving ready-made answers to these questions, it's best if parents step back and support teenagers in deciding for themselves. For example, if your son approaches you and asks you whether he should do French or History as an exam subject, it may be best for you not to give an immediate answer, but to ask 'What do you think yourself?' 'What do you think are the pros and cons for each subject?' This way, you encourage your son to work out this decision for himself and prepare him for making adult decisions later on. Stepping back and letting teenagers evaluate decisions and consequences about their lifestyles can be difficult when you don't agree with some of their decisions. For example, it may be difficult to step back and listen first when your thirteen-year-old daughter says she wants to get her nose pierced, or if your fourteen-year-old son wants what you think is a crazy haircut.

TAKE TIME TO TEACH YOUR TEENAGER

You can't suddenly hand over responsibility to teenagers without taking time to teach and prepare them for it. We often assume teenagers know how to do basic chores when no one has taught them. Just because they have watched you do the laundry or the ironing for many years doesn't mean they have learnt how to do it themselves! It takes skill, tact and time to teach someone something in a way that empowers and motivates them. This is the difference between nagging a child to mow the lawn, which they eventually do badly, and teaching a child an appreciation of gardening over time so that they mow the lawn better than you and take pride in the result. In preparing children to take responsibility for a task, it can be helpful to take time to:

1. Explain clearly what has to be done. Give them an appreciation of the purpose of the task.
2. Ask them what help they will need from you in order to learn the task (For example, you can demonstrate what has to be done, or you can do the task together, or you can let them go off and do the task and come back to you to report progress, or you can do all three in sequence).
3. As far as possible let them make choices in how the task is done. For example, you don't mind when your daughter does her ironing and washing, as long as it is not in the living room. For some tasks you can encourage your teenager to be creative (for example, on your son's night to cook, you let him surprise you with the menu!).
4. Make your teenager accountable for the task, getting credit if it is done and experiencing consequences if not.

ALLOW TEENAGERS TO LEARN FROM CONSEQUENCES

Responsibility means experiencing the good and bad consequences of our actions. Just as it is important to let teenagers take credit for achievements and take pride in a job well done, it is also important to let them experience what happens when things go wrong, so they can learn from their mistakes. Parents can often rescue teenagers by covering for them when they don't do their homework, or giving them pocket money even though they did not complete the expected chore, or ironing their shirt at the last minute even though they can do it themselves. Letting teenagers experience consequences and learn from mistakes is not abandoning them; rather, it is teaching them to take responsibility for their actions. Even in doing this, you can still be encouraging and on their side, helping them learn, but you are not there to take over and rescue them. Consider the following example:

Thirteen-year-old Joe wanted to leave the football team. He didn't really enjoy it and just wanted out. Bob, his father, was worried. Joe didn't do much physical activity and didn't have many friends. He was worried that Joe would be 'moping around' the house, bored, for the summer. He listened to Joe, expressed his concerns, but Joe was adamant that he wanted to leave. In the end, Bob did not object but supported Joe in making his own decision. Sure enough, during the summer Joe began to complain that he was bored, that he had nothing to do and no friends to hang out with. Bob didn't react righteously with an 'I told you so' (though he felt like it); instead he bit his lip and empathised with how Joe was feeling. Being listened to, Joe was able to admit that he 'sort of regretted' leaving the football, though he still wanted to do something different. Bob told him that it took courage to face regrets and he asked Joe would he like some help in thinking what to do next. Joe readily agreed and together they found a different sports club that Joe made a commitment to attend.

MAKE TEACHING FUN

Teaching a teenager a new task does not have to be boring and formal. The more you make it fun and enjoyable, the better. For example, you can ask your son to do a six-week cookery course with you in the autumn; or offer to decorate your daughter's room with her and use the time to teach her painting skills; or you can suggest a family spring-cleaning day (followed by a big family treat), when each teenager chooses a special task but when you all work together. Such shared activities are often times of great connection between parents and children.

START SMALL

It can be a big transition to change to be an empowering parent. If you are a parent who does everything for your teenagers, it can be difficult suddenly to relinquish all your jobs, and your teenagers doubtless would not be prepared to take them on. It is best to start small and to pick out something that you are going to teach your teenagers to do over the next week. Perhaps you are not going to wash up every evening yourself but ask your children to do a night each, or you're not going to take responsibility to get them up every morning, or to do their laundry. Whatever you decide, it's best to sit down and explain in advance that you want to begin letting them take some responsibility for household chores and family tasks, explaining the benefits of this. Listen to their ideas and views (you may be surprised that they are very reasonable) and explain your own ideas and conclusions. When you do start this new approach, expect some resistance and teething problems. Teenagers may agree to do tasks but find it hard to follow through and take responsibility. In addition, they are bound to test your word to see if you really have changed, and it is important that you keep your resolve. They need to discover that if they don't do their own laundry, then nobody will magically step in, and they really will have nothing to wear on Saturday night!

TIPS FOR GOING FORWARD

1. Pick a family task or household chore that you want to hand over to your teenagers.
2. Sit down and talk to them, explain why you want to hand it over to them (e.g. a fairer system, teaching them responsibility).
3. Agree to teach them the task if needed.
4. Agree on the rewards for doing the task and the consequences for not.
5. Arrange to talk again to review how they got on.

Step Seven – Negotiating Rules and Boundaries

One evening fifteen-year-old Paul tells his parents that he wants to stay over at his friend Bill's house for the forthcoming Halloween night. His parents, who have only met Bill twice, are unsure, and they tell Paul they want to speak to Bill's parents first. Paul doesn't want this, saying it would be 'humiliating'. He wants his parents to trust him instead.

What decisions should teenagers make for themselves and what rules and boundaries should parents establish? What are reasonable rules to have for teenagers and how do you enforce them in a way that teaches self-responsibility?

This section gives some suggestions as to how parents might negotiate and follow through on rules with their teenagers, a process that, when handled correctly, can teach a young person responsibility and build mutual respect between parent and child. We build on all the valuable skills already covered (such as pressing the pause button, listening during conflict and speaking up assertively) and add three further important stages:
1. Negotiating and agreeing rules
2. Agreeing on consequences
3. Following through

Negotiating and Agreeing Rules

Remember the 'Big Picture'

Parenting is a very long-term task. The goal is to help teenagers to learn how to be responsible adults who confidently make their own decisions. Rules should be seen as a flexible set of guidelines and agreements that are established to help navigate this long parenting journey. Good rules allow children to take responsibility for their actions and to learn from their mistakes. You don't want a set of rules that over-controls a young person, meaning that they never learn things for themselves. Nor do you want no rules or boundaries at all so that a young person is exposed to unnecessary risk and has few guidelines to learn from. You want rules that protect young people, but that also let them learn and begin taking more responsibility for themselves.

Involve Young People in Deciding Family Rules

Negotiate, negotiate and negotiate. These are the three most important principles in agreeing rules with teenagers. The more they are involved in the discussion, the more you listen to them, the more you try to accommodate their views and wishes, the more likely they are to respect and uphold the rules. The process of negotiation can take a lot of time. It involves lots of discussions, lots of one-to-ones and possibly lots of family meetings. Busy parents can often be tempted just to impose a rule or make a quick decision. However, this overlooks the benefits of negotiation. The process of negotiation ensures that you as a parent remain appropriately involved in your teenagers' lives. It gives you a chance to connect with them and to communicate your own values and feelings. In addition, it teaches young people how to express themselves and to think through their own opinions and values. It is certainly worth the time.

Rules work best when they are family agreements that everyone was involved in creating and that everyone tries to keep. For example, if you're concerned as a parent about the amount of TV your kids watch, rather than simply imposing a rule such as 'No TV before 6pm', why not spend some time (perhaps in a family meeting – see Step Eight) discussing the issue, highlighting the benefits and dangers of TV, and try to come to an agreement. Remember, this could take time and lots of listening (and several meetings!), but if you arrive at an agreement, you have achieved a priceless piece of work in teaching responsibility.

KEEP 'NON-NEGOTIABLE' RULES TO A MINIMUM

Parents often make the mistake of having too many rules for their teenagers, which can lead to conflict and rob teenagers of the chance of making their own decisions. For example, do you really have to insist that your daughter tidies her room to your standards or can you close the door and let her take responsibility? Or you may not like your son's haircut, but maybe it's best not to make an issue of it, and let him decide how to cut his hair. While there are times when you have to make rules that your teenager doesn't agree with, these should be kept to a minimum and reserved for really important things. It helps to think through in advance what rules are really important to you as a parent. Often families sit down and come up with these together. Such 'non-negotiable' rules might include:
- No drug-taking
- Letting you know where they are
- Not travelling alone at night
- Friends welcome but only when an adult is in the house

Even when you do make a rule that your teenagers are unhappy about, it is still important to talk it through with them and to listen to their point of view and feelings. In addition, teenagers can be helped to accept a rule when they are given choices about how it is enforced. In the example at the beginning of the chapter, the father could help fifteen-year-old Paul to accept the rule by giving the following choice:

I'm sorry Paul, but if you want to stay over at your friend Bill's house, then I want to ring his parents first to check it's OK. I understand that you find this a bit embarrassing but I need to know you will be safe. You may want to tell his parents first that I'm going to ring if that is easier for you – that's your choice – but I need to talk to them before you go.

Agreeing on Consequences

You won't be surprised to hear that even though you can reach well-thought-out agreements about rules with your teenagers, they will still break them. The route to self-responsibility involves lots of challenging and testing of limits. For this reason, it is best to have thought through in advance the consequences of rules being broken and agreements not being respected. These work best if they are reasonable and fair and if the teenager has been involved in deciding them. Discussing consequences with teenagers in advance gains their co-operation and treats them as accountable adults. Ask your teenagers what they think should be the fair consequence of breaking a rule or an agreement. You may be surprised that they will generate better and more effective examples than what you thought of yourself!

Examples of consequences include:
- If Rob is an hour late coming in, then he has to be in an hour earlier the next night.
- If Sue does not do her chores for the week, then either she has to do double chores the next week or she doesn't get her pocket money for the week.

- If James does not arrive home for a family dinner, then no cooked meal is available for him.
- If Orla does not get up early enough, then she has to walk to school without a lift.
- If Peter does not do his washing and ironing, then he has no clean clothes on Saturday.
- If the washing up rota is not working, you will discuss it again at the next family meeting.

The last consequence is a particularly important one. If the agreement is not working then it will be discussed again rather than forgotten about and abandoned. Knowing that there is a review time, when they will be accountable to other family members, is a powerful motivating factor for teenagers to 'get their act together' and to do what they promised. The style of the meeting should be exploratory and not punitive. The aim is to understand what happened and brainstorm how to move forward to solve the problem.

Even with serious problems, establishing consequences with teenagers can help them take responsibility for their actions. Often these consequences can be given as choices to teenagers. For example:

Parent: I can't sit by and let you use drugs with your friends. I'm too concerned about you. Either you choose to stop meeting your friends at the club or you come with me to see the drugs counsellor.

Parent: If you get suspended from school, then you stay in at home and study for the period you are suspended. You won't be allowed out or to play computer games.

FOLLOWING THROUGH

Following through is essentially about you as a parent keeping the promises and agreements you have made with your teenagers, so that they learn to do likewise. It is about not giving in and ironing your son's shirt for him at the last minute because you feel sorry for him, or taking your daughter in the car when she's late for school, when you agreed before that she should take responsibility. Keeping these promises can be hard on parents, which makes it important only to make agreements and consequences that you know you can keep yourself.

When following through, it is best not to make a fuss about it or use it as an opportunity to lecture your teenager, for example, 'I knew you would not be able to get up on time – it is typical.' Instead, try to be calm, firm and matter of fact. You can even be supportive, but do not rescue. For example, it is okay to say when your son misses an agreed family meal, 'I'm sorry you're hungry', but it would be a mistake to make him a special meal.

In addition, if you agree that a rule (e.g. a chore rota) will be reviewed at a later date, for example, at a family meeting, it is important that this meeting does in fact take place and that you don't avoid the discussion for fear of upsetting your teenagers or inviting trouble. By keeping your side of the bargain, you model responsibility and make teenagers accountable for their actions.

Tips for Going Forward
1. Make a list of the really important rules you want kept in your house (This can be a great exercise to do with the whole family).
2. Negotiate the exact form of these rules with your teenagers and what the consequences are when rules are not kept.
3. Be sure to follow through on any consequences you agree.

Step Eight – Solving Problems/Talking Things Through

The secret to getting along with your teenagers and reducing conflict is in finding better ways of communicating with them – finding ways to listen and to get through to them. While this is true of all children, it is especially true of teenagers, who are developing more of an adult relationship with their parents. Most of the ideas in this book have been geared towards improving communication within families. Good communication is the basis for solving problems. Connecting with teenagers, finding out about their worlds, listening and speaking to them in the good times, give a basis for talking things through and solving problems during the rough times.

FAMILY MEETINGS

One way families can keep connected and keep the lines of communication open is to organise regular family meetings. Family meetings are special times set aside for all the family to attend. They can be used to talk together about important issues, have fun, make plans (such as for holidays), negotiate family rules (such as how much TV to watch, or who does the washing up), etc. Meetings run best when they are run democratically, with a special emphasis on trying to reach consensus or 'win-win' agreements. Though parents might initially lead, it can help to alternate the role of chair and give someone else the task of writing down decisions, and another person the responsibility of keeping track of time.

Once family meetings become established in a family culture, they can have a transforming effect. Many parents describe them as invaluable in completely altering the tone of family life from one of conflict and distance to one of co-operation and closeness. Family meetings give a routine way for parents to stay connected with their children, to listen to their concerns and to

share their own views. However, parents also report that family meetings can be difficult to establish in a family, especially with teenagers who are initially suspicious or cynical about the process. Drawing a teenager into participating can take time but it is well worth the effort.

DRAWING TEENAGERS INTO FAMILY MEETINGS

1. *Introduce the meeting as important but informal.*
   Rather than making the meeting sound very 'formal', it can be helpful to introduce it in a matter-of-fact, informal way. For example, 'I thought it would be a good idea if we could all have a meal together on Thursday. It would also give us time afterwards to discuss the summer holidays. I want to hear your views on where we should go.'

2. *Make meetings relevant to their concerns.*
   Make sure the meetings address issues that matter to the teenagers (as well as issues that matter to you). For example, if your daughter says she feels she's lumbered with all the household chores, or your son approaches you saying he wants a TV in his room, rather than solving these disputes there and then, say 'Why don't you bring it up at the next family meeting?' If these are issues that they feel strongly about, they are likely to attend and participate.

3. *Share power during the meeting.*
   Attending family meetings is usually attractive to teenagers once they see that it is a forum where they will get a 'fair hearing' and

49

can have an input in how family decisions are made. For this reason, share out power in the meeting. Encourage teenagers to take the role of chair or note-taker from time to time.

In addition, 'go slow' during meetings. Decisions can be postponed until the next meeting if there is not enough time. The main focus is on listening and understanding, making sure everyone has a chance to air their views.

4. *Make meetings fun and not all work.*

   A lot of families end their meeting with a game or a special family activity that everyone enjoys. Children can be given turns in selecting the activities.

5. *Don't make meetings compulsory.*

   Don't get into a power struggle, forcing a teenager to attend a family meeting, as this can defeat the purpose. Instead, strongly encourage them to attend, making it attractive for them to do so. Let them experience the consequences if they don't attend, for example, not being there when important decisions affecting them are made, missing out on a favourite meal and a fun time.

6. *Persist with drawing them in.*

   Don't worry if teenagers come with an 'attitude' or appear little interested from time to time, which is quite normal. Instead, persist with respectful communication on your part. Even the most 'switched off' teenager can open up eventually and participate.

SOLVING PROBLEMS

The mark of a healthy family is not whether they have problems or not, but whether they go about trying to solve them. What counts is being able to sit down and talk through the problems as they arise. Once a family is able to do this they can get through most of the difficult times they encounter. Below is a six-stage model you can use to solve problems. This model can be used 1) during a family meeting when everyone is present, or 2) with an individual child, or 3) with your partner when you have a difference of opinion, or 4) even by yourself to think through a dilemma you have. The six stages are:

1. Connecting/setting time and space aside
2. Listening first
3. Speaking up respectfully
4. Thinking up solutions
5. Choosing the best solutions/making agreements
6. Meeting again/follow up

The first three stages have already been covered, and indeed the basic skills of connecting with teenagers – listening first and speaking up respectfully – are often sufficient in themselves to solve problems. This is especially the case with listening. The source of most conflict between parents and teenagers is misunderstanding and lack of trust. Once this is resolved through empathetic listening, much of the conflict dissolves and solutions can naturally flow. Stages Four to Six describe how solutions and agreements can be established.

THINKING UP SOLUTIONS

Once you have understood your teenager's point of view and expressed your own feelings, you are now in a position to think up or 'brainstorm' with her possible solutions to the problems you are facing. Rather than simply giving your own solutions it is important to hold back and first encourage your teenager to come up with ideas and ways forward herself. This can be done by asking questions such as: 'How do you think you can solve this?', 'How can you ensure you get home on time?', and 'How can you convince the teachers that you're trying a little harder?' Though it is tempting to come up with your own answers, it is crucial to proceed at the teenager's pace and to wait for her to generate the solutions. Solutions generated by teenagers are far more likely to be carried through by them. You will be surprised at how even the most 'difficult' teenager, when given time, can come up with solutions that are as good as or even better than those thought up by parents. Parents can add their own ideas and suggestions, but this is best done after your teenager's ideas have been explored or when she specifically asks you for suggestions.

At the brainstorming stage it is important to generate as many alternative solutions as possible – the more you have the better. It is also important not to be critical at this stage; encourage your teenager's creativity and listen to all the ideas she comes up with. These can include solutions tried successfully in the past. You can help your teenager recall times when things were going better or the problem was solved. For example, you can ask 'How have you solved this in the past?' or 'Do you remember last year we had the same problem, but we got through it. How did we do it then?' Once talked about and understood, these past solutions are more easily repeated.

CHOOSING THE BEST SOLUTIONS/MAKING AGREEMENTS
Now it is time to help your teenager decide which solutions she is going to use. During this stage the emphasis is on helping teenagers think through the consequences of the ideas suggested in the brainstorming stage, in order to identify those that have the best results for both them and other people. Frequently, teenagers come up with unrealistic or inappropriate solutions. However, rather than criticising, you can guide them by asking them to think of the consequences. Asking questions like 'What do you think will happen if you try that?' can be helpful. For

example, as a way of avoiding a bully, a teenager might suggest dropping out of the school team. But on thinking it through, he realises that this could leave him feeling like a failure and would mean him losing out on being part of the club. With the support of his parent he may come up with a different solution, such as confronting the bully or gaining the support of the other boys to do something about it.

MEETING AGAIN /FOLLOW UP

When the best solution(s) is/are chosen, it is important to arrange a time to talk again to review how things are going. This is a crucial and often forgotten stage. Solving problems takes time and often many attempts, and persistence is needed to make a breakthrough. If an attempted solution doesn't work out, it is important to meet again to find out what happened and to support your teenager in finding a new course of action. Even if things do work out, meeting again gives you a chance to encourage and compliment your teenager, and this can be very empowering to them. In addition, by meeting again and thus following up on agreements, you make your teenagers (and yourself) accountable and thus encourage them to take responsibility for their actions.

PROBLEM-SOLVING IN ACTION

Let's look at how this problem-solving model can work. We will continue the example introduced in Step Five, where fifteen-year-old Lisa is discussing with her father, Bill, the idea of leaving school. After initially flying off the handle, Bill pressed the pause button and set aside a time to talk to Lisa. He first listened as she spoke of her struggles in school, and then he expressed his concerns about her leaving early. In the dialogue below, they go on to look at possible solutions.

BRAINSTORMING/THINKING UP SOLUTIONS

Bill:	I just wonder, if things were a little different at school, would you be able to turn things around?
Lisa:	I don't know.
Bill:	Well, what would help?
Lisa:	Well, it's mainly Irish and History that I get into trouble in.
Bill:	Maybe we could look at getting extra help for those classes.
Lisa:	Or maybe I could get out of doing them altogether, and just concentrate on the others.
Bill:	Maybe, we'd have to talk to the principal about that. . . . What could you do to help?
Lisa:	Well, I could try to keep out of trouble and to work harder.
Bill:	That might help.
Lisa:	I also still wonder whether I would be better leaving and getting an apprenticeship.
Bill:	That is another possibility.
Lisa:	Or if I did leave, maybe I could study at home and still do the exams.
Bill:	Possibly.

Notice how at this crucial stage Bill encouraged Lisa to come up with solutions herself. He did not criticise her ideas, but encouraged her to identify as many potential solutions as possible. The aim at this stage of problem-solving is to be creative and to work with your teenager to generate lots of ideas and possibilities.

CHOOSING THE BEST SOLUTIONS

Bill:	So we've got a few ideas then. We could try to get you extra help for the classes, or talk to the principal about reducing the time you spend in some classes, and you could think of how to keep

	out of trouble and work a bit harder. Or you could look at leaving school at some stage and either seeking a job, or maybe doing the exams while at home. What do you think?
Lisa:	I'll try to give it another go at school. Maybe we could talk to the principal, but I'm not sure it will work.
Bill:	We can still look at the other options. It's probably a good idea that you look at what you want to do when you leave school anyway – whether this is sooner or later. It would be good if you could leave with some exams.

REVIEWING HOW YOU GET ON

Bill:	How does that sound?
Lisa:	Okay.
Bill:	We'll talk again about it next week.

While in real life problem-solving may take a lot longer, especially for a difficult issue (and that is why it is crucial for Bill to meet Lisa to talk again), the above example illustrates the different steps you can take to talk through problems with young people.

TIPS FOR GOING FORWARD

1) Set aside a time to talk through a problem with your teenagers using the six-stage model described in Step Eight.
2) Rather than immediately giving solutions, remember to hold back and to help them generate their own solutions. Listen to their ideas first and add yours later.

Step Nine – Parents Caring for Themselves

There was a man working furiously in the woods trying to saw down a tree. He was making very little progress as his saw was blunt and becoming blunter with each stroke. The man was hot and frustrated and continued to work harder and harder. A friend of his noticed what was going on and he asked him, 'Why don't you stop for a few minutes so you can sharpen your saw?' 'Don't you see,' replied the man, 'I'm too busy sawing to take any time off.'

Stephen Covey[4] uses the above story to illustrate the futility of working non-stop and the importance of parents taking time off for rest and relaxation to renew themselves. So many parents become martyrs to their children, devoting all their time and energy to the task of parenting, without thinking of their own needs and wishes. Other parents become excessively focused on the problems and conflicts they have with their children and all their energy is spent in disagreeing with their children or correcting and rowing with them. In both these positions, not only is the parent liable to 'burn out' from stress and exhaustion, but their parenting becomes increasingly counter-productive and negative. In the first example, the parents can become resentful and/or can become run down, with little energy to relate to their children in a consistent, loving way. In the second example, the correcting approach is liable to increase the power struggle between parent and teenager, and may lead to more rebellion, until either the parent gives up or the teenager walks out.

As the story above suggests, it is crucial to take time out to 'sharpen the saw'. Parents should 'press the pause button' and take time to look after their own needs as well as attending to the needs of their children. When parents' own needs for care, comfort and fulfilment are met, they are freed up to attend fully

4 Covey, 1997

to the parenting role. Children need cared-for parents as much as they need parents to care for them. The best way to help your children grow up to be confident people with high self-esteem is for you as their parent to model this – that is, to take steps to value, love and prioritise yourself.

You may protest that in your busy life you simply can't afford to take time out for yourself. The reality is that you can't afford not to. Think about the times you have been run down or exhausted or feeling low and how it was impossible then to do any of the 'more important' tasks. Remember the times you felt energetic and good about yourself and how easy it was then to achieve things and to be kind and loving to others. A little a bit of self-care goes a long way.

HOW TO SHARPEN THE SAW

Self-care and personal renewal are basically about achieving balance in your life. They are about trying to ensure each week that you address your different needs in a balanced way. There are four dimensions of self-care and personal renewal that we need to address weekly in order to have a balanced and stress-free life.

1. Physical
   Exercise (such as walking, jogging, playing sports)
   Eating well and healthily
   Getting good rest and relaxation

2. Mental
   Keeping your mind stimulated with other interests (such as reading, movies, theatre, etc.)
   Learning new things

3. Emotional
   Keeping in contact with friends
   Connecting with intimate family (e.g. special night out with partner)
   Doing self-nurturing things (e.g. treating yourself to a special bath or a shopping trip)

4. Spiritual
   Time alone/time in nature
   Time for personal reflection
   Meditating, prayer
   Goal-setting, reconnecting to your values.

The aim of self-care is look after your greatest asset in creating a happy family life – you. All the ideas in this book can only work when a vibrant, motivated and cared-for parent is there to implement them. Caring for yourself as a parent is really the first, or the most integral, step in making a difference to your relationship with your teenager.

FAMILY RENEWAL
Taking time out to sharpen the saw is something that applies equally to family life. Healthy families find time to renew and recharge themselves. Much of what has been described in this book is all about renewing and rebuilding family relationships.

For example, we have described connecting and sharing with family members, spending quality relaxed and enjoyable times with one another, listening empathetically, and expressing our own feelings. All these activities 'sharpen the saw', for individual family members and for the family as a whole. Ensuring you have regular quality time, by yourself, with your partner, with your children and with your family as a whole, can be a way of not only eliminating stress but also finding personal meaning.

TIPS FOR GOING FORWARD

1. Set aside a special time next week, just for yourself, doing something you really enjoy.
2. Plan to spend special relaxed time with your partner away from problems next week. If you are a single parent, do the same with a close friend or other family member.

FURTHER READING

Covey, S. R. (1997). *The Seven Habits of Highly Effective Families*. London: Simon and Schuster.

Gottman, J. (1997). *The Heart of Parenting: How to Raise an Emotionally Intelligent Child*. London: Bloomsbury.

Murray, M. & Keane, C. (1997). *The Teenage Years*. Dublin: Mercier.

Nelson, J. & Lott, L. (2000). *Positive Discipline for Teenagers*. Roseville, California: Prima Publishing.

Quinn, M. & Quinn, T. (1988). *What Can a Parent of a Teenager Do?* Newry: Family Caring Trust.

Sharry, J. (1999). *Bringing Up Responsible Children*. Dublin: Veritas.

FOR GROUP LEADERS

Sharry, J. and Fitzpatrick, C. (1997). *Parents Plus Progamme: A video-based guide to managing and solving discipline problems in children aged 4-11*. Parents Plus, c/o Mater Child Guidance Clinic, Mater Hospital, North Circular Road, Dublin 7.

Sharry, J. and Fitzpatrick, C. (2001). *Parents Plus Families and Adolescents Progamme: A video-based guide to managing conflict and getting on better with older children and teenagers aged 11-16*. Parents Plus, c/o Mater Child Guidance Clinic, Mater Hospital, North Circular Road, Dublin 7.